Through Rose-Colored Glasses

Poetry In Motion

October 6, 2007

Best Wishes. Enjoy!

Ahsai Morris

Through Rose-Colored Glasses

Poetry In Motion

Alison Morris
Destiny Publishing

Another book by Alison Morris:

Imani's Song: A Collection of Poetry For The Mind, Body and Spirit

Copyright © 2004 by Alison Morris

All rights reserved. No part of this book may be reproduced or transmitted in any form or by any means, electronic or mechanical, including photocopying and recording or incorporated into any information retrieval system without written permission from the author, except by a reviewer, for the inclusion of brief passages in a review. Permission requests should be sent to:

Destiny Publishing
P.O. Box 217
Mount Pocono, PA 18344

Morris, Alison

Through Rose-Colored Glasses

Poetry In Motion

ISBN: 0-9702745-1-3
Library of Congress Control Number: 2004090848

Manufactured in the United States of America

First Destiny Publishing Edition

Dedication

In Memory of Sister Graham

"From your lips to God's ears."

Acknowledgments

I must begin by thanking and praising Jehovah Jireh-- my provider, my God, who has given me everything I needed for this journey.

My heart becomes heavy with gratitude when I think of the numerous family members and friends who have been supportive of my work over the years. This book was a distant vision, yet it was through the encouragement and eager audience of family, friends and at times total strangers, that it became a reality. To all of you, and you know who you are, I say thank you. In fact, I can't thank you enough. After embracing my first book, *Imani's Song,* you continued to look for the next one, never giving me a chance to rest, but constantly asking, "Are you working on another book?" And so, it is partly because of you, the dedication and support that you have extended to me, that this book exists.

A very special thank you is extended to my mother Elise Morris, for her undying support. To my dear friend, Ana Hazell, thank you for your commitment in sharing my work both near and far.

For the many people who were touched and liberated through my poetry, I say thank you for the opportunity to come into your lives and share my work with you. I feel blessed and I now know that this is what I was destined to do. My life will never be the same again.

Contents

Part One - Rhythm of Life

My Soul Started Singing	15
Lifeline	17
Nature's Symphony	18
The Writer Within	19
Oasis	20
Open Your Eyes	21
My Prayer	23
He Sees All	24
Use Me	25
Living Waters	26

Part Two - Growing Pains

Monday	29
My Imitation Alligator Boots	31
May I?	34

Contents

Misery Loves Company	36
Traveling Shoes	38
Extend Yourself	41
Faith Walk	42
Turn It Around	43
The Dwelling Place	44
Born Rich	46
Someone Is Crying Tomorrow	47

Part Three - Color My World

Land of the Free	51
The Only Thing I Changed Was My Hair	54
Somebody Just Snatched My Pocketbook	56
The Cross Over Generation	59
Profile, Please	62
Waiter, Oh Waiter	64
Black Mother's Prayer	67

Contents

Prince	70
The Lost Tribes of Africa	71
Don't Forget The Code	73
A Rose	74

Part Four - Freedom

She Never Raised A Murderer	77
Jungle Fever	79
A Special Day	81
Hello Sun	83
This Life	85
A Wealthy Place	87
A Perfect Gift	88
Heaven's Angels	89
She's Still Here	90
Womanhood	93

Part One

Rhythm of Life

My Soul Started Singing

There was no special reason,
No surprise call
from a distant friend
No unexpected flower delivery
But, I felt good all over
I mean, all over I felt good

I just couldn't figure out why
There were no checks in the day's mail
Trees were swaying and
it was quite chilly outside
Yet, there was unexplainable joy
deep, down, inside of me
I'll never forget the day
It was the day my soul started singing!

All day my soul sang
It had to be something good coming
I mean, something real good was on the way
Just like a child on his birthday,
I was excited, with anticipation
Excited, as I listened while my soul sang

It woke me up singing
And sang all day and into the night
I felt so good
I wasn't sure, I'd be able to sleep

But just in time
It turned into a lullaby
and my, oh my
I knew a blessing was coming
And a blessing was already here
Right there inside of me was a soul!
That could feel good things
before I could see them
Connected to the universe
it knew what would be
before it came to be
So amazed was I
and grateful to be alive
I just smiled and shouted
Sing, Soul, Sing
Sing On
With Your Bad Self!

Lifeline

This pen and paper has rescued me
It has been a lifesaver
A buoy in the ocean
An anchor in rough seas

What would I do without it
When there is nowhere to turn
and the pain is unexplainable
completely unbearable
there it is
Beckoning me, inviting me to come
to release everything trapped inside

After filling all the empty spaces
with pain and confusion
After purging my soul
of heartache and despair
Bringing emotion to the surface
and creativity to the paper
I emerge relieved
comforted
at peace

This pen and paper that costs so little
yet means so much
has saved my life

Nature's Symphony

On a fine Spring day
I listened as...
The wind whistled between the leaves of the trees
The birds sang to their heart's delight
Water babbled down the streams
And bees buzzed as they pollinated the flowers

I watched as...
Baby ducks quacked while swimming in the lake
Wild geese soared above, calling to everyone below
As I sat, listened and watched,
I was warmed by the sun's presence
This was certainly Nature's Symphony
What a wonderful performance!

The Writer Within

As an artist creates from nothing

Something beautiful

So do I, gather words

into a colorful bouquet

which heightens the senses

while beckoning you

to read on

Oasis

Find a place that brings you joy

Where even in the midst of chaos

you find peace

Allow yourself time to restore wholeness,

while your world may be crumbling apart

Close your eyes and breath deeply

while thinking positive thoughts

Transform your life

You deserve it

Open Your Eyes

When sadness engulfs my spirit
and the seasons of my life
turn from bright summer
to cold winter
I weep
thinking
no one understands
no one cares
feeling alone
and in great despair
I close my eyes
and cry
rivers of tears
while searching for a way out
And right there in the midst of it all
A small voice whispers,
"Open your eyes."
Through vision blurred from tears
is evidence of blessings;
clothes
food
shelter
Blessings
Giving me the strength to stand

"Open your eyes," whispers the still small voice.
There are sights and sounds I took for granted
Birds singing

Trees changing
The peace and quiet I cherish
Giving me the power to walk

"Open your eyes," I gently hear.
Taking a deep breath
I smell the freshness of the wind after a rain
While soothing my body
it's lifting my spirit

Breathing deeply I feel the crisp air
helping me to feel better
Right there in the cold harsh winter of life
I believe I can make it
just one more day
Remembering those simple words:
Open Your Eyes

My Prayer

Give me strength O Lord
To fight battles both big and small
Give me power O Lord
To defeat the enemies that attack my very soul
Give me wisdom O Lord
To discern the good from the bad
Give me knowledge O Lord
Spark in me a new way that the world
has never seen
Give me patience and understanding O Lord
recognizing my own faults
while accepting those whose lives are different
Then, use me O Lord that your grace and love
may shine

He Sees All

As a youngster, I learned
God sees all

No matter where you are
Or what you're doing
God is watching us

He's in the heavens
way up beyond the skies
from a distance so far away
He sees all

He gives only what he wants you to have
and no more
Sometimes the heavens pour out
an over abundance
Sometimes you barely have what you need

He knows about your situation
while bringing you through
the most difficult of times
Rest assured
God sees all

Use Me

A gift from God is unmistakable
It is like a flower bursting forth as a seed
Deep beneath the ground
It is formed with strong roots
and mighty strength

In the midst of darkness
it grows despite many obstacles
Through winding paths, it shoots upward
Despite rocks and pebbles in the way
it continues on it's course

Even when rain floods the surface
The same water brings forth nourishment,
guidance, power
Just when that seed begins to feel weary
it breaks through the surface
receiving light and warmth from up above

There is no place to go but up
Nowhere to branch except out
Revealing a magnificent gift
A flower from heaven

Living Waters

When the world has depleted the essence of soul
Go to the waters and be filled
Bring all trouble and confusion
Carry all pain and sorrow

Release it all
Empty, purge, eliminate
Go wide and deep
Be cleansed by the waters
Bring rest to body, mind and spirit

As the tranquility of the pond's water beckons,
stand still
As the harmony of the lake's water summons,
be renewed
As the vastness of the ocean's water invites,
be filled

Wait no more to inhale
hesitate no more and exhale
Breath now; renewed, refreshed

The world awaits you

Part Two

Growing Pains

Monday

Heard about a man
who hadn't worked for three years
three years
didn't pay rent or mortgage,
car note or insurance
bought no clothes
food, gifts, were luxuries
time was limitless

He was laid-off, downsized,
fired and unemployed
Even with the classified ads, networking,
resumes and interviews
He found no work
no work for three years
He hadn't worked for so long
that he was
looking forward to Monday
Monday
when he could
wake up and get up
shower, dress and have breakfast
Monday
when he would travel, to get there
work his shift
go home
and talk about the day

He was looking forward to Monday
and the things it would bring
Paying his bills
A place to live
Food to eat
Clothes to wear
For him and his family
and maybe a little extra
to do something nice for someone else
to save for a rainy day

He got a call one day
and worked for ten years
without a sick day
ten years
and was never late
best employee on staff
Every Sunday, He looked forward to Monday
and all the things it would bring

How long would it take you?
To look forward to all the things
you take for granted
To look forward to Monday

My Imitation Alligator Boots

In 1970, I had them.
BOOTS
ALLIGATOR BOOTS
Not, ALLIGATOR BOOTS
But, IMITATION ALLIGATOR BOOTS

My so-called friends told me exactly what they were
As they pointed and laughed,
whispered and snickered,
"Here she comes, with those
IMITATION ALLIGATOR BOOTS
Ha, Ha, Ha, He, He, He."

I thought they were fine...
at first.
Mmm...
Black - - easy to polish
High - - came up to my knees
Fur lined - - would keep my legs warm
Alligator Print - - fashionable
So we bought them
Mom and I
They looked fine and fit fine
Until my friends, (so-called) saw them
Then came the laughter and snickers,
pointing and whispering

It was then that I learned that my boots
were imitations
They were plastic, not alligator
even the fur inside, was imitation fur

But I continued to wear them
they kept my legs warm
and taught me so much

For now, years later...
when people laugh and snicker,
point and whisper
I am reminded of those
IMITATION ALLIGATOR BOOTS

I am warmed by the imitation fur
Insults bounce right off me,
and I know, it was the plastic, not alligator
Wearing those boots strengthened me
I know they were on my feet,
but my backbone became stronger

And people, they always have something
to laugh and snicker,
point and whisper about...
if it's not my hair or my skin,
it's my clothes or shoes

I just smile, knowing that
it looks fine and fits fine
I wear it well, whatever it is!

So Mom, I want to thank you,
thank you, thank you
For making me wear
MY IMITATION ALLIGATOR BOOTS

May I?

Sometimes life can really take you down
and when you think you can get up
it will knock you down again
and again
and again

You rise slowly
before putting one foot
in front of the other
You ask carefully
humbly
"Father, May I take one giant step?"

And then you recall
the days of yesteryear...
when you were playing
with your neighborhood friends
You hear,
"No, you may not, you may take
one itsy, bitsy, baby step!"

You laugh, remembering
the number of years that have past
and how it was just a game
we played a long time ago
and move you must

You move very cautiously,
carefully,
remembering that life
has knocked you down before
and may do so again
With wobbly legs and shaky knees
you step and step
Yes, itsy, bitsy, baby steps
While you get back on track
with steps that were ordered,
prepared just for you

As you put the pieces of your life back together
from whatever it was that has knocked you down
again and again
You notice that those knees and legs are stronger
You can stand longer,
step farther
And from this day forward
in all that you do
remember to ask,

"Father, May I?"

Misery Loves Company

It was a love affair like no other
The two of them were inseparable
Walking hand in hand through life together
Yes, Misery loves Company

Misery loves that horrible feeling
of being down more than up
Misery loves chaos, confusion,
and constant complaining
Misery says, "Let me count the ways
to make your life a terrible ordeal,"
while whispering nothing else in your ear.
Misery is not content in feeling bad alone
and so the search begins for a companion
Someone to share all those negative thoughts
and deeds with
Yes, Misery loves Company

For drama is not drama
unless you have someone to share it with
So, morning, noon and night
the phone rings off the hook
and who's calling?
Misery with gossip
Misery with turmoil
Misery with trouble

Misery never calls with pleasant news,
sends cheerful letters in the mail
or arrives at the door with a bouquet of flowers

No, there must be tears, grief and gloom
Misery never arrives and leaves alone
True Misery
Loves Company

Traveling Shoes

For two years prior
and four years thereafter
they would be my closest companions

That's how long it took me to get them
and to keep them
There were no others!

They were with me
through thick and thin
good times and bad
through tears of joy and sorrow
My true supporters

My Traveling Shoes

Tell me...
What woman do you know
who owns only one pair of shoes?
One Pair
To take her to
weddings and funerals
meetings and conferences
court appearances and speaking engagements
One pair
To travel to
parties and church
dinners and shows

One pair
blending with every color outfit
and giving no pain despite
the many miles of walking

They were made just for me!
Comfortable
A Perfect Fit

My Traveling Shoes

They were admired by many
Always polished, buffed and shined
Folks often wondered
where the money came from
for the house, the car, the business
– It came from the shoes!
Discipline – Sacrifice – Hard Work
It was the shoes!
And there was only one pair

Four years and only one pair
Think of the money you could save
There's the house, and the car, and the business
It's in the shoes!

So
When they retired
I knew it was time to move on
and when they were laid to rest
I felt the loss and grieved immensely

reminiscing about all that we had been through
My closest companions

My Traveling Shoes

Extend Yourself

Have you helped someone today?

Have you given of yourself in a thoughtful way?

Have you extended a hand to someone in need?

Think about it, and do just one good deed

There's someone nearby who could use a friend...

to walk with

to talk with

to laugh and relax with

So before the day is over

give of yourself

take the time to do something nice

for someone in need

You'll be amazed to see

how the world will be a better place.

Faith Walk

Step out on a promise
Believing that it will become a reality
Each day move closer to the goal

Concentrate on your heart's desire
Knowing that only death could keep you from it
No matter what comes your way,
Keep focused on your dream

Hold fast to your vision
It's yours for the asking
You can make it happen

Turn It Around

A glass of water is precious
Long walks essential
Changing our eating habits are vital
To prolong our lives,
while improving our health

Never knew how important
a good night's sleep would help
Never gave it a second thought
A good laugh is soothing to the body
Positive thoughts can transform your world

In a land of plenty
filled with so many choices,
endless possibilities
Be selective
Love yourself
You are important
Change the course of your life
Do it today

The Dwelling Place

Don't stay in a place
Where life gets you down
Where you rise in the morning
with yesterday's headache
Where present troubles consume
every waking moment
Don't Dwell There

Though turmoil rises
to the boiling point
and anger has taken residence
on the inside of you
Let it go
Move on
Don't Dwell There

Don't stay in a place
Covered with blankets of pain
Filled with closets of sadness
Draped with curtains of fear

Feel the tears only for a while
Allow yourself time to heal
Give yourself permission to release it
Then, let it go

Get up
Shower it all away
Eat with a new attitude
Dress with a desire for brighter days ahead
Move on
Step out
Please, Don't Dwell There

Born Rich

Imagine having so much money
you could buy anything your heart desired
So rich you didn't need health insurance,
car insurance, home maintenance contracts
You would pay everyone with cash
and go to the specialist of your choice

You're so rich you could live
wherever your heart leads
and buy anything you desired
Would there be a reason to work
to get rich or to stay rich

In the absence of money, are you rich?
Is there love inside and around you?
Do you wake each morning feeling blessed
to be alive?
Do you have family and friends that care about you?
Then you were born rich

Is your health holding on for just one more day?
Can you pour nourishment into your body,
mind, spirit?
Can you touch someone's heart with a warm gesture
or kind word?
Then you were born rich
Make today a good day and remember
You were born rich

Someone Is Crying Tomorrow

On this very day
for the rest of their lives
they will remember
The tragedy that occurred
which changed their lives
and shook the very foundation of the earth

It is a day of mourning
for tomorrow they know
tears will flow
Rivers of tears
uncontrollable, unrestrainable
Like a dam in the midst of a flood
Like a waterfall after a storm
Tears will flow

On this day, year after year
they will remember tomorrow
The panic, fear and worry
the sadness that never seemed to end
for their loved ones
who left one day
and never returned

As sure as the sun shines
As sure as a new day dawns
Someone _is_ crying
tomorrow

No doubt
No question

Tomorrow
Faces will turn into streams
Overflowing streams
filled with tears of grief
tears of sorrow
Crying for their loved ones
while remembering a day
they can never forget

As this day turns to night
someone is preparing for tomorrow
the day of remembrance
a day when the earth stood still
the day of reflection
September 11th

We will always remember!

Part Three

Color My World

Land of the Free

There are two worlds
in this country
One White
One Black

One Rich
One Poor
The Haves
and The Have-Nots
A stranger feels it
A citizen knows it

It stretches as far as the eye can see
From mountains high and valleys low
From sea to shining sea

Where prejudice looms
and inequalities reign
In this land of the free
Built with the hands of the slaves

Where one day, Miss Lily,
put on her rose-colored glasses
and confidently stepped out proud and tall
with dignity and grace

She strutted right into a magnificent hotel

where generations earlier her grandmother
would have worked as a maid
The elegance and grandness of the lobby
caused her eyes to twinkle with glee
All was right with the world
until her bubble burst
right before her eyes
When the reservation was lost
(So they said)
And the two, double bed, no smoking room
was unavailable
(So they said)
They offered her one bed and a cot
and the smoking room didn't smell so bad
(So they said)

They encouraged Miss Lily to go
and smell the room
In other words, sniff around like a dog

Remembering her ancestor's struggles
caused Miss Lily's legs to become strengthened,
her back erect
So, she stood in silence.
Contemplating, whether they were
prejudice, ignorant or both

She stood in silence...
It must have been a computer error
(So they said)

When the entire room mess
was finally straightened out
Miss Lily checked into
the two, double bed, no smoking room
and rode in a sparkling, immaculately clean elevator
remembering the day when her grandmother
would have rode in the cargo elevator
with the other servants
She stopped short of singing, We Shall Overcome
Cause Lord knows she was tired
of singing that song
and we should have overcome by now
Especially here in this Land

Where even in the year 2000 and something
racial profiling, police brutality and segregation
are alive and well in America
and straight through to Canada
Hard to believe there was ever an underground
railroad on this route

She removed those rose-colored glasses
and saw the world as it was
instead of how it should be
It wasn't a pretty picture
She was comforted by her ancestor's
indomitable spirits, strengthened by their struggles
and warmed by their triumphs
while she laid herself down to sleep
hoping that one day in her lifetime
a change would come.

The Only Thing I Changed Was My Hair

Even though years had past
I wore the same clothes
I was a little older, calmer, and much more patient
So, I was surprised at this sudden change in attitude
As always, I was neatly dressed, not flashy at all
so that wasn't it
The color of my skin had not changed
so that wasn't it
I still spoke English with clarity and intelligence
so that wasn't it

Yet I couldn't put my finger on
the constant racial confrontations...
Once, I was accused of stealing an item
purchased at another store
Accusers said they saw me pick it up and walk
right out of the store
(It had to be wishful thinking)
Twice, airline employees kept my luggage for days
before returning it
(I suppose the drug sniffing dogs
gave them the o.k.)
And when they refused to take off
until all the passenger's I.D.'s were checked,
they started with mine, ended with mine,
and checked no others in between
(I still can't figure that one out)

So I looked at myself in the mirror last night
and noticed that very little had changed
In fact, over the years,
the only thing I changed was my hair
It's Locked
Tendrils
Glistening with pride and distinction
Absolutely Beautiful, if I must say so myself

I now look like the women, I admired for so long
Those women, not afraid to be who God
 intended them to be
ALL NATURAL
Confident
Beautiful, African women
Adorning Harlem to Tanzania
Completely comfortable with who they are
So this, is a change I welcome
and for those who have a problem with it,
I wave my hand and say,
"Whatever!"

Somebody Just Snatched My Pocketbook

I work hard for my money
saved every penny, nickel and dime
So I went down to the car dealership
and happily picked out the car of my choice

I barely sat down in the car
when just that fast
somebody snatched my pocketbook
stealing over three hundred dollars
before I even had a chance to blink

The salesman overcharged me on the sales tax
But wrote nothing on my contract
Just used his calculator
and told me what the tax figure would be

He could have...
Hit me over the head
kicked me in the stomach
knocked me to the ground
and pulled my pocketbook from my arms
Cause that's what it felt like
when he stole my money

Corporate criminal
Custom suit wearing hustler
Standard English speaking thug
that's what he is

I told him to keep the car
and had to fight to get my deposit back

White Collar Criminal
There should be a law!

And just when I thought that was cleared up
I woke up one day and my pension was gone
Gone
My job was gone
and all my money went too

No one came out with anything
except the people at the top
they saw it coming
and came out with everything
They cashed in their stock options, 401 k's
and took early retirements
Laughed all the way to the bank

I...
cried till no more tears came out
shouted, stomped
cursed and cursed some more

Cause my pocketbook was gone
and all my money went with it

It wasn't snatched by a group of boys
hanging out on the neighborhood corner

They were well-educated
in the art of robbery, treachery and deceit
They received an A-plus
in falsifying documents
withholding crucial facts
and shredding potential evidence

Masterminds? No
Criminals!
Clear and simple.

There should be a law!

But, there is.

Unless, of course
your collar is White.

The Cross Over Generation

They're a new generation
Destined to be different from all the rest
A select group
Wise, shrewd, outspoken warriors
Slightly ahead of their time
The elders don't understand
what they are doing or why
Only God knows...
They are preparing to cross over

To change the course of history
as we know it
To rise as leaders, heroes
for a new day
with a fresh way to view the world
They are a radical bunch
Bold, Courageous
The Cross Over Generation

They speak when they're not spoken to
and question those in authority
Looking eyeball to eyeball
Standing toe to toe
Shoulders erect
Confident, unwavering in their position
to change the course of life
as we know it

Be he Nat Turner
or Jesse Jackson

Harriet Tubman
or Al Sharpton

The pendulum swings
back and forth in time
as it identifies individuals
and groups of people
who push forward and fight
beckoning the generation
to be different from the rest
To Cross Over

To stop abuse in the family
To produce college graduates
instead of high school dropouts
To reach farther than anyone has gone
And envision bigger possibilities in life
To own land
homes
businesses
To liberate themselves
by any means necessary

Crossing over every line drawn in the sand
Crossing over the thresholds of doors
that were once closed
Defying the invisible boundaries
which separate them from their destiny

They are the cross over generation

Be he famous
or unrecognized
They are in your family
or on the airwaves
charged with a lifelong task
long before they were ever conceived
raising above adversity and controversy
They are destined for greatness
and prepared to cross over

Profile, Please

It's driven by fear,
deep rooted fear
of those who are different
They look different
and speak differently

Based on fear...
a group is outlined
Dark skin
African
Arab name
Female
Asiatic features

Based on fear...
they are stopped
at airports
on highways
in stores
on our streets

Based on fear...
they are rounded up
searched
humiliated
detained
incarcerated

This so-called security measure
which strips basic human rights
instilling anger, distress, resentment
fueling divisiveness
perpetuating racism, sexism and hatred

Based on fear...
of those who are different
simply different

They are lined up
beaten verbally, physically
fingerprinted
recorded
photographed
as they stand erect,
turning to the left
and then to the right
while the camera man says, "Smile,
profile please."

Waiter, Oh Waiter

Traveling has never been easy
But traveling and eating is even harder
So we rode for miles
hundreds of miles
and found only one nice place to eat

We sat down
waited and waited
waited and waited some more
Finally, hungry and tired
we were served, by our waiter
burnt home fries and cold eggs
with a smile and a bottle of ketchup

This was our welcome
into the new millennium
Could have fooled us,
looked more like
Mississippi in the early 60's
where signs read, "No Coloreds Served Here"

We looked at one another
and did a double-take
Same clothes
Same hair
Hue still Black
Money still green
So we sent it back

was not worth a stomach ache
two nickels rubbed together
or a penny on the bill
We traveled on

We rode through winding roads
and around steep trails
ended up in the middle of nowhere
Hungry, tired and ready to eat

We walked through the restaurant doors
and found all eyes on us
From the maitre d' to the patrons
We were clearly on stage,
but too tired to play the part
So we gave our name to the hostess, and waited
Since reservations were not required
they were never made

So we waited and waited,
waited and waited some more
And though all the guests who arrived before
and after us were already seated,
we checked our name to make sure
that it hadn't disappeared from the list
Realizing we were there to stay,
we were seated and served
Food was exceptionally good

We paid with a charge card
and received the third degree

Never knew a piece of plastic
could cause so much commotion
Waiter said they had never heard of the company
So what else is new!
Yes, this must be Alabama in the 50's.
where some folks were never extended credit

Must have been a reason for the full to half-full rule
for the gas tank
And the fried chicken and bread in a shoe box
for a just in case snack

Just in case you're hungry and can't find a restaurant
willing to serve you

Welcome to the new millennium!

Black Mother's Prayer

Heavenly Father
Hear My Prayer
Out of my womb
birthed life into this universe
a spiritual being
preparing for a worldly experience
I know that you will provide everything
needed for this journey
And as I dedicate my child's life back to you
I ask that you watch over my baby

Lord, protect my boys
As I name them one by one
Pour love, compassion, and wisdom into his spirit
Shower him with strength, power and discernment
to face life's challenges
Fill him with the gentleness of a lamb,
the strength of a warrior
and the wisdom to know when to use it
Watch over him as he travels to and fro
at home and in unfamiliar places
Surround him with a hedge, a fence
Keep him day by day from dangers seen and unseen
As life's temptations approach him
Give him a do right mind
To live in a manner which pleases you

Lord, protect my girls
As I name them one by one
Surround each with your mercy and grace
Give her a clean heart
Remove all jealousy and envy
Replace it with empathy and love
Help her to be all that you have intended
And encourage her to reach for the stars
in all that she does

Lord, watch over my children
Rid them of illnesses and suffering
that consume their bodies
Heal them
Keep them off the streets
where trouble abounds at every corner
As they grow, guide their steps to higher learning
Create a way out of no way
for them to build a sweet life
out of sour lemons tossed their way
Level the playing field
while granting them what they need
to push forward
Order their steps back to you, dear Lord
To serve you
And depend solely on you
For all that they need

And Lord, when my life is over
When my last song is sung
It is my desire that you will see my sacrifice

in my offspring and be pleased
I thank you this day and everyday
for providing us with everything we need
and so much more
For it is a blessing to know one another,
love one another
and be connected in this time and place
It is to you that I am most grateful
for this opportunity
I thank you and I count it all done
In your majestic name
Lord, hear my prayer

Prince

He's the direct descendant of royalty
Royalty
Imagine that!
Five generations ago
his ancestors arrived on the shores of America
Chained, shackled, whipped and bruised
Speaking an old language in a new land
Five generations of torture followed
by savages,
who felt they had rescued savages,
to work as slaves for over 200 years

He's the direct descendant of royalty
Proven only now that he's made millions
for someone else
and little for himself
Now that he's risen above it all
Surviving, in spite of it all
Proving himself to be a true warrior and conqueror
He stands before us as royalty

His blood line has been traced
his family tree in now complete
From the shores of America
To the village in Nigeria
Five generations of hardworking entrepreneurs
He's royalty
Imagine that!

The Lost Tribes of Africa

An explosion is occurring across America
A move so huge, it hasn't been seen in generations
Doors are opening from state to state
to welcome them home
Those who have been scattered for so long
The tired, the hurting, the broken-hearted
The sons and daughters of tribes divided
They are finally home
Singing praises
Dancing in the footsteps of King David
Being restored, renewed and set free
While their spirits are liberated and families mended,
from years of turmoil and strife

Welcome home
To churches and temples
all across America
As they have weekly reunions of families
once forgotten
Seats once empty are filled to capacity
Doors once closed, now opened
Mega congregations
with lines down the block
and around corners
just for a chance
to worship and praise
A mighty God

From the shores of Africa and the Carribean
to America's land
The sons and daughters of tribes once lost
now meet
at the most segregated hour in America
Sunday 11 o'clock

Don't Forget The Code

The zip code
Five digits, sometimes nine
Which determine:
where your children go to school
the attending hospital in cases of emergency
how much government money
your community receives

So powerful are those numbers
They decide:
if your home is on the good or bad side of town
whether your car insurance will increase or decrease
if businesses will deliver to your home after dark
or at all
where you will be directed
for municipal sponsored programs

Lest we forget
Those special numbers:
determine segregation or integration
Not only is it the color of your skin, now
It's all in the code

A Rose

To see the world through another dimension
as a place much different than what it is
Our vision is colored
like that of a sweet smelling rose
Life is the way we want it to be
Our vision stays that way
Until we remove the glasses
with rose-colored lenses
Revealing the truth, the reality
of so many things we prefer would just go away,
disappear
racism
sexism
poverty
hatred
hunger
war
We walk through life with our glasses on--
the color of sweet smelling roses
pretending that it's not as bad as it is
and believing one day perhaps
the problems would just go away

Part Four

Freedom

She Never Raised A Murderer

It was twenty-one years ago today
she held her baby in her arms
while rubbing her face softly against his
She savored the moment
and dreamed of what a blessing he was
and would be to everyone
Mother thought good thoughts
as she loved and cared for him
from day to day

Who would have thought that today
of all days
she would be riding a bus
to the state penitentiary
to visit him...
her son, her baby
Who would have thought
that today
he would be given a new name
murderer, thief, rapist

What a wonderful child he was
only ten years ago today
as he helped around the house
ran errands for the neighbors
and tried his best at school
He was warm and friendly

sweet as apple pie
with a smile that could light up a room

As her heart began to ache
and she couldn't blink the tears away
sadness engulfed her spirit
even her head seemed too heavy
to hold up
because she knew
she never raised a murderer
nor a robber, rapist or drug dealer

No, she raised someone special
giving the best she had to give
and loving him with her whole heart
That's who she raised

As she spoke to her son
behind bars
the avalanche of tears
couldn't stop flowing down her face
and she remembered just fourteen years ago today
who she raised
that polite, considerate,
happy and often giggling little boy
Yes, that's who she raised.

Jungle Fever

Nothing is more important than a lioness
protecting her cub.
Be it in the lion's den or on the plains
a secure and loving environment
is always number one.

She will do anything, at anytime
for her baby
It is the law of the jungle!
An innate part of her being.
A mission charged to her by the creator
So, it is normal and quite understandable,
the inferno which emerges
when her cub is in distress

She shakes her hair, believing this can't be...
Grunts, snarls and pants excessively,
with shear fury
She arches her back and points her nails
in preparation for the attack
She fights for her cub with an undying power
continuous resilience
and emerges seemingly tireless from her defeat
Be it with her lion or an anonymous intruder

Armed with the fruits of her struggle
her cub rejoices
with jubilation and glee

There is food, shelter, clothing
all the support a child needs
The den is secure once again
And when the lion...
or an anonymous intruder
asks the lioness,
"So what do you want out of all of this?"
The lioness simply pauses while she smiles
and grooms herself
from the recent battle and replies,
"A drop of cold water is all I need."

A Special Day

Woke up this morning
with a smile on my face
with a song in my heart
as I remembered a very special day

It was only yesterday
and the memories are already precious
From sun up to sun down
we enjoyed ourselves
We laughed, smiled and giggled
rolled down grass covered hills
made sand castles at the beach
dug up worms to catch fish at the lake
and watched stars
while drinking lemonade at night
We didn't spend a nickle or a dime all day
not a penny or a quarter all night

It was a special day
"A No Spending Money Day"
From dawn to dusk we used only what we had
And enjoyed the free things in life
It's still hard to believe
But we had so much fun
We'll have to try it again
Perhaps one day a season
Maybe even one day a month

As fall approaches,
we'll play all day and into the night
Football, baseball, basketball,
hockey, skating, and bike riding
Not having two nickels to rub together
won't matter on that day
it will be a special day
"A No Spending Money Day"

During the winter we won't use a dollar or a dime
to create a delicious lunch,
using only what's in the house
We'll build snowmen with carrot noses
go sledding down hills,
make angels in the snow
and drink hot chocolate when our hands get too cold

We'll have a good time
on these special days
Every season of the year
And best of all it won't cost us a dime
It will be, "A No Spending Money Day"

When spring approaches we'll start all over again
Not worrying if our pockets are empty or full
We will focus on what brings us joy
With a bag full of ideas to last the whole season
Each day will be, "A No Spending Money Day"
For the best things in life really are free

Hello Sun

With wars erupting
all over the world
fighting between nations everyday
over land, money, oil
and sovereign control of the people
Isn't it nice to know that we share the Sun
The Sun, so far away that we can still see it's splendor
and feel it's warmth
It lights up the earth
and ignites creation every second of the day
It's energy is free for the asking

So, as I watched footage from the war
in Israel and Palestine
I couldn't help but look up
at the dawning of a new day
when the Sun's rays shot across the sky
bringing serenity to a war torn land

It's extraordinary power
unparalleled to anything we can imagine
It's energy and intensity
can make a strong man, weak
It's heat knows no boundaries
and cannot be claimed by anyone

While nations find reasons to fight
over borders, people, money and oil
They can't fight over the Sun
Thank God there's something
we all have to share
Gracious Sun
We Welcome You!

This Life

Thought my life was immortal
Believed I would live forever
But just as the flowers die, so will I
As sure as the snow melts
one day I will fade away

Put my life on hold
defying the law of time
Believing that I would be here tomorrow
that I would have just one more day
Yet, as day turns to night
I will go
Just as the seasons pass before my eyes
One day I will see no more

Never thought so much about this
Wanted to move on to happier things
But death can never be denied
Someone is with you one day
and gone the next
As the circle of friends shrink
As family members fall by the way side
The realization of life becomes pronounced
The facts of death unavoidable

As surely as you were born
you will die

Just as the midst flows on a rainy day
so will I pass away

Never wanted to think much about this
Never gave it a second thought
Yet, as I celebrate each new day
I know that one day
night will come.

A Wealthy Place

There once was a country so wealthy
that the dogs were treated
with more love, respect and kindness
than was ever known to men

Dogs received pedicures
and their coats were regularly groomed
pampered and fluffed
The finest foods were often set aside
for dogs
Yearly doctor visits were common place
and medicines amply available for dogs

Yet, in a country so wealthy
elderly people sometimes ate food fit for dogs
Yes, dog food
Many had to choose between
food or medicine
because they couldn't afford both
So, many elders traveled to Canada
for affordable medicine
They were too old to work
and too poor to pay
In a place so wealthy
Is it any wonder why the young
never wanted to get old

A Perfect Gift

Love
Builds a wall of protection around you
while creating a bond so strong
it can never be broken

Love
Forms a connection you can depend on
No matter what the circumstance
you know it will always be there

Love
Creates a sense of security
Instills a feeling of well being
Fosters care, concern and warmth
It costs nothing and can last a lifetime

Love is
the best gift anyone could ever give

Heaven's Angels

So many people today are preparing to die
Preparing to move over to the other side
They are ready to enter a new dimension
and to be with those
that have journeyed before them

They have stepped into a phase of life
unimaginable to many
They plan and direct
their own funeral arrangements
Locate the will and distribute the inheritance
Visit all the relatives and close friends
preparing them for the inevitable,
the day they will journey home
The peace and inner strength is amazing
They say no more to surgery
                       medical procedures
                       medicine
They say things like, "Let me go,
I've had a good life."
Demanding to leave the hospital and go home
to rest and wait for the day they will journey
It is a difficult thought for everyone involved
Yet, it restores dignity to death as we know it
And prepares us to rejoice for the homecoming
that is sure to come when they journey home

She's Still Here

Who is the person in your life
that surrounds you with unconditional love
and support?
In my life, it's my mother
and I'm so glad that she's still here.

Still here
transcending the boundaries of time,
while embracing me with undying love

Still here
providing a channel
through which the spirit of God
can travel to the generations to come

Still here
believing that I could conquer
any challenge which comes my way

Still here
exuding power, strength and dignity

Still here
to help me make it through one more day

Whether we are near or far
Whether seen or unseen

Our spirits are connected
Like a cord that can never be cut
Like a chain never to be broken
Defying the obstacles of life
Building a bond that will never go away
We are one against the world
Creating a strong family line
As we transfer life's lessons
from Queen to Princess
and then Queen to Queen
She's Still Here

Still here
to pour wisdom and knowledge
into my spirit

Still here
in an ever evolving relationship
sometimes clashing, while times change
and also our views about the world

Still here
to alert me to dangers I cannot see

Still here
providing support and building me up
when some want to tear me down

Still here
seeing me at my worst,
while revealing that the best is yet to come

As Queen Mother imparts to Queen
all that is needed to make it on this journey
with a love so strong, it transcends time itself

I know I'm blessed
And I'm so glad
that She's Still Here.

Womanhood

The weights of life had me down
I didn't know it
I had carried the weights on my shoulders
for so long that
I didn't even know it

I walked around
did the dishes
raised my child
cleaned the house
went to school
even drove the car
with those weights on my shoulders
Bar bells – Heavy loads
And I didn't even know it

Slowly... as the weights were being removed...
I felt it
My burdens were being lifted up
off my shoulders
My left side felt lighter
and then my right side
It felt great!
It felt exhilarating!
Even the air smelled different
As I was being lifted up
out of the valley

and I didn't even know
I had been down
Hallelujah!

My knees no longer buckled
My ankles no longer quivered
My back began to straighten
And I learned how to balance
in reverse
as the weights were being removed
slowly--from the right side
and then the left
the sweat, I wiped from my brow
--and all those years
I didn't even know I was sweating

It was the greatest balancing act
of all times
--Being a Woman
Hallelujah!
I feel like singing!

Order Form

To purchase additional copies of *Through Rose-Colored Glasses* by mail, complete the information below and send it to:

Destiny Publishing
P.O. Box 217
Mount Pocono, PA 18344

The cost of *Through Rose-Colored Glasses* is $11.95 plus $2.00 shipping and handling per copy. Pennsylvania residents must add 6.00% sales tax. Make check or money order payable to <u>Destiny Publishing</u>.

Name_____
Address_____
City_____State_____
Zip Code_____
Telephone # (Optional)_____

Number Of Copies_____